MURPHY'S
LAWS
OF FISHING

MURPHY'S LAWS
OF FISHING

HENRY BEARD

ILLUSTRATED BY PHIL SCHEUER

Sterling Publishing Co., Inc.
New York

A JOHN BOSWELL ASSOCIATES BOOK

Library of Congress
Cataloging-in-Publication Data Available

2 4 6 8 10 9 7 5 3 1

Published by Sterling Publishing Co., Inc.
387 Park Avenue South, New York, NY 10016
© 2007 by Sterling Publishing Co., Inc.

Distributed in Canada by Sterling Publishing
c/o Canadian Manda Group, 165 Dufferin Street
Toronto, Ontario, Canada M6K 3H6
Distributed in the United Kingdom by GMC Distribution Services
Castle Place, 166 High Street, Lewes, East Sussex, England BN7 1XU
Distributed in Australia by Capricorn Link (Australia) Pty. Ltd.
P.O. Box 704, Windsor, NSW 2756, Australia

Printed in China

Sterling ISBN-13: 978-1-4027-4776-2
ISBN-10: 1-4027-4776-4

For information about custom editions, special
sales, premium and corporate purchases, please contact
Sterling Special Sales Department at 800-805-5489
or specialsales@sterlingpub.com.

design Nan Jernigan

INTRODUCTION

BACK IN THE early days of recreational fishing, when the basic code of piscatorial behavior was first established ("If you have to hold it with tweezers, it's not a keeper"; "Let the bear have the fish"; "Never pee into the wind"), there simultaneously appeared, pretty much out of nowhere, a series of shrewd and rueful observations about the gentle art of angling that were nearly always attributed to a mysterious individual named Murphy.

As time passed, these canny precepts ("If something can go wrong, it will, and at the worst possible time") and savvy admonitions ("If it ain't broke, don't fix it") found their way into the worlds of business, the military, government, science, and economics. But the roots of the by now legendary Murphy's Laws clearly lie in fishing, a sport that seems to have been tailor made to expose the fundamental malevolence of the cosmos.

For where else but on a trout stream or a bass lake or a charter boat or a seaside pier could anyone so swiftly conclude that nature is not simply indifferent but actually hostile, and that, far from being blind, fate has superb eyesight and a mean streak a mile wide? After all, long before the paradoxical principles of quantum mechanics were discovered, anglers had already had ample opportunity to experience the sheer perversity of the universe firsthand: they watched in baffled disbelief as outboard motors refused to obey even the simplest laws of mechanics, lengths of casting line became tangled in all eleven of the dimensions predicted by superstring theory, favorite lures got stuck in globs of antimatter at the bottom of tackle boxes and were instantly vaporized, and schools of hungry lunkers swam into time warps and started feeding like crazy the day before yesterday.

Whether Murphy was an actual historical character and the two hundred and fifty axioms, maxims, laws, and dictates that bear his name truly are the work of some solitary Einstein of the rod and reel is almost beside the point. Whatever their source, these astonishing nuggets of fishing wisdom represent one of the greatest contributions to the understanding of the sport ever made and taken together provide a foolproof guide to its manifold frustrations.

Well, almost foolproof. This book, like everything that fishermen and fisherwomen encounter (and just about anything that anyone else does) is subject to the unforgiving effects of Murphy's great theory, and so, if there are any misprints, or upside-down pages, or any other laughable boo-boos, please accept in advance the auther's sinecrest appologies.

Murphy's
AXIOMS OF ANGLING

There are a whole lot of fishermen, but surprisingly few catchermen

The person you had to drag kicking and screaming to the lake, stream, or shore will catch all the fish

The only really unbearable quality in a fishing buddy is the ability to catch fish when no one else can

Patience is a vice

Sisyphus' brother was Fishyphus

Luck is skill displayed by another angler

An expert angler is someone who has learned to avoid all the minor, commonplace fishing errors and can proceed directly to one colossal boner

The only thing you can learn from your mistakes is how to make them quicker

Unsolicited fishing advice is the only thing that is every bit as welcome as a cold, hard, steady rain

Anything worth doing better be worth undoing, too

Unlucky is temporary; stupid is forever

There is no fishing mishap so dire that it cannot be remedied with the use of a properly functioning time machine

It isn't a serious problem if it can be solved with a sharp knife or a bald-faced lie

The only way fishing could be trickier would be if water could catch fire

In the midst of any fishing crisis, always ask yourself, How would the Creature from the Black Lagoon have handled this?

For an angler to do something truly stupid, mere incompetence is not enough; you really need an audience

If you accidentally hook another angler, don't insist on having him weighed for a possible record

A lot more people would take up angling as a sport if there were some way to bet on the fish

Fishermen probably aren't crazy enough to put in a mental hospital, but if they end up in one, no one would let them out

In fishing, the role of Mother Nature
is always played by Joan Crawford or Sissy
Spacek

As fishermen go, Captain Ahab was
pretty laid-back

No fly-fisherman ever looked half as
good as Brad Pitt, including Brad Pitt

A fool and his money make excellent fishing companions

Never take a check from anyone who uses a fishing license as I.D.

What do you expect from a pastime where the very first thing you do is open a can of worms?

Murphy's
SCIENCE OF ICHTHYOLOGY

The little bubbles in the stream are caused by fish laughing

All fish will bite like crazy under certain specific conditions, except when they don't

Fish will never bite until the last hour of the day, unless you arrive in the last hour of the day

A fish is a keeper if it weighs more
than the gear used to catch it

Ten out of every four fish that got
away were almost certainly trophies

There is no limit on lost fish

The reason fish have teeth isn't so
they can smile at you

The only contest you can always win
with a fish is a game of "keep away"

A fish is just a very roundabout way
of tricking you into eating worms

The difference between tenacity and idiocy is one damn fish

A ton of fish weighs about three pounds

Two fish are a bunch

The quickest way to find out exactly how much line you have on your reel is to hook a trophy fish

Your chances of ever catching a record fish increase in direct proportion to your distance from a reliable scale

Trout will take any lure so long as it's at the end of a tangled line

Bass bite best during a backlash

Fish get the weekend off, too

Lunkers are irresistibly attracted to ultralight tackle

Trash fish never break off

The surest way to get fish to bite in any particular spot is to leave it

All fish feed sooner or later, but it's
sooner than you can get there and later
than you can stay

If the fish are biting, you can catch a
salmon with a lollipop; if they aren't biting,
you can't catch a bluefish with a pork chop

The reason fish jump when they throw the hook is because they can't give you the finger

If you want to think like a fish, you really need to drink like one

The most likely reason fish are so temperature sensitive is that by now they all have enough mercury in them to function as thermometers

Murphy's
TENETS OF FISHING TECHNIQUE

You can't catch bass without a six-pack

Any simple, efficient, inexpensive,
and productive method of catching fish
will be considered unsporting

Even if you hand-tie the fuses and
execute a really stylish throw with a
smooth continuous side-arm motion,
it is never sporting to fish with dynamite

A bird in the hand is evidence of a very wild cast

Never ask a fly-fisherman if he really thinks trout live in trees

The art of casting can be easily mastered by anyone with three good hands

The reason why so many former golfers take up fishing is that the basic motion used to make a cast comes naturally to anyone who ever threw a golf club

If you somehow manage to get the fish into the barrel, there's really no need to shoot them

There are three basic types of fishing: catch-and-release, hook-and-cook, and stop-and-shop

Before you release a fish, decide whether you're going to go for style points or distance

Never release a fish with topspin

If you're too squeamish to kill a fish by bopping it on the head with a club, you can always bore it to death with the story of how you caught it

It's easy to gut a fish if you clean out the insides of a beer first

It's no big deal to clean a bunch of fish if you've already decided to remodel the kitchen

It's not that simple

It takes much longer

It costs a lot more

If you ate it, it's a keeper

It isn't poaching if you fry it

You never need to clean the one
that got away

Even if the fish broke off fifty feet from
the boat, it's always the fault of whoever was
holding the net

Look on the bright side—you haven't
lost a fish, you've found a reason to buy
a new piece of fishing equipment

Murphy's
RULES OF THE LURE

If a lure doesn't work today,
try it yesterday

If the wrong lure works, it's most likely because you cast it badly

There are two basic types of fly-fishing lures: the ones that should have floated, and the ones that were supposed to sink

If you can't remember where your thumb is, try looking in a pile of hooks

The shortest distance between any two points is a finger

The other lure is always best, unless it's the other other lure

When putting bait on a hook, always leave room for the fish

No live bait is worth a damn unless you threw up when you put it on the hook

The only way to know for sure that a particular lure will work is to lend it to someone fishing next to you

No matter how lousy the lure, there's always a worse one you can change to

The only way to make absolutely
certain that a knot will not come loose is
to try to untie it

The reason you can't find that sinker
you're looking for is because it's the larval
stage of all those swivels and snaps you
have far too many of

You should have set the hook right away, unless you did, in which case you should have waited a little longer, but if you had, you wouldn't have waited long enough, but it doesn't really matter because it was the wrong hook, and even if it had been the right hook, you would have forgotten to sharpen it

Any old lure can catch a rock

Snags are always biting

Weeds aren't choosy

The farther you are from a fish, the easier it is to get the hook out of its mouth

The less it looks like a fish, the likelier a hook is to catch it

There are two ways to tie a fly: the wrong way and the other wrong way

It takes no more skill to tie a fly than to arm-wrestle a polka dot

If the fish were trying to catch us, their favorite lure would be a shiny, new boat

The people who design lures know they aren't bought by fish

Fool me once, shame on you; fool
me twice, shame on me; fool me three
times, go open a bait and tackle shop

Remember, in the bait shop,
you're the fish

It is no more difficult to make a fly-cast
than to toss a pound of noodles through
the mail slot of the house across the street

Murphy's
THEORY OF BOATING

Never let an outboard motor
know you're in a hurry

The likelihood of an outboard motor malfunctioning is in direct proportion to its distance from the shore

The odds against an outboard motor starting double with each successive pull of the cord

The best way to get an outboard motor to start on the first try is to forget that you have a stringer of trophy fish hanging off the back of the boat

Boats never leak in shallow water

Two wrongs make a canoe

There is no such thing as a free launch

If you ever have to bail water out of a boat, the only container available for the purpose will be an empty aspirin bottle or a 40-gallon drum

There will be a completely edible boat before there is a truly portable one

There is enough room in a skiff for one fisherman or two former fishing buddies

If you don't think fishing is a contact sport, spend a day in a party boat

The only way to be sure that the water is deep enough for a boat is to try to fish it in waders

If you're going to use an electronic depth finder to spot fish underwater, why not just go ahead and declare war on the bastards, force them to the surface with depth charges, and then ram them with your boat

The more a piece of equipment costs, the less likely it is to float

The only happier day than the day you
buy a boat is the day you find some sucker
to sell it to

The only thing that will not instantly
corrode, rust, or dissolve in salt water
is taffy

If it ain't broke, you ain't bought it yet

The odds of your catching a fish are in inverse proportion to the expense and complexity of your fishing gear

The intensity of an itch is inversely proportional to its accessibility

A pair of waders is a remarkably powerful laxative

If you leave it alone, it will fail

If you mess with it, it will break

If you throw it overboard in disgust,
it will float

They don't make it anymore

There is no substitute

Somewhere there's a guy with
600 of them in his garage

A device that performs more than two functions will do all of them poorly

There are two basic screwdriver designs: the one you have and the one you need

There is no knife so dull that it can't cut a finger

You can do just about anything with
a pair of nail clippers except find them

Paper runs out; scissors get lost;
rocks break everything

There is nothing so small that it can't
make a loud noise, or so large that
you can't forget to bring it

All warranties scrupulously honor
their expiration dates

All repairs are temporary

No improvement ever is

Broken tackle attracts fish;
functioning cameras spook fish

It takes an awful lot of tackle to lose
a single fish

If you wonder why fishing gear is called
"tackle," leave some of it lying around

A whole lot of bad knots have just as much holding power as one good one

All knots are just a tangle with a name

Never let a knot know you're running out of line

The easiest way to get the sections of a fishing rod to come apart is to pray they don't

You cannot fix one part of a piece of fishing gear without breaking some other part

It is perfectly possible for a fishing line to be too long at one end and too short at the other

It is nearly impossible to find a hidden fracture in a rod without the assistance of a very large fish

Tape either won't stay on
or won't come off

Things either won't open
or won't stay shut

What goes around comes unwound

Glue works best on fingers

All sticky liquids are claustrophobic and
can't stand being cooped up in little bottles

Spare car keys eventually dematerialize
if they aren't used regularly

An hour of good fishing takes all day

The week before you came, the weather was perfect; the week after you leave, it will be even nicer

Bad days come in bunches; good days are packaged individually

A 10% chance of showers can hit 100% of where you are

The shortcut isn't

90% of casts are into the wind

All paths leading to fishing holes are
uphill, and so is the way back

There is no truly effective rainblock

You never run out of fish repellent

The only thing that is truly waterproof
is a fish

Hatches always happen in the past tense

The best tide is always at three in the morning

If the bugs aren't biting, don't worry — your luck is bound to change

The preferred habitat of trout is directly under a bridge from which fishing is prohibited, or along the banks of a stream that runs through land owned by someone who doesn't fish and hates fishermen

The perfect fishing spot is anywhere you're not

April showers bring May floods

Every cloud has a cloud-colored lining

It never rains on Monday

One's a crowd

It takes two to tangle

The fish are always someplace else,
unless you're someplace else, in which
case they're someplace elser

Deep water looks a whole lot like shallow water

To a leech, you're a keeper

Murphy's
PRECEPTS OF THE FISHING TRIP

Next time, come last week

A fishing trip of a thousand miles
begins with a single wrong turn

Your fishing equipment will always be the
first piece of luggage down the carousel at
the wrong airport

No flashlight ever went dead on a bright, dry, warm moonlit night

If you brought it, you won't need it; if you need it, you definitely didn't bring it

In fishing, if you let your conscience be your guide, you're going to catch crapola

Always keep in mind that as soon as he shows up, your guide has already caught his fish

The act of removing any item from the bag specially designed to hold it immediately increases the volume of that item by a factor of two and reduces the capacity of the bag it came in by 50%

Matter can be neither created nor destroyed, but if you put it in a backpack, it's going to get larger and heavier

The only tent that is ever big enough
is one with a circus in it

Never in the entire history of the world
has there been just one mosquito

People who snore fall asleep first

A fire that was next to impossible to start last night will be next to impossible to put out in the morning

The animal noises you hear at night are seldom made by bunnies

If you think it's a bat, it's a bat; if you think it's a big moth, it's a bat; if you think it's a loose tent flap, it is whole lot of bats

A fishing trip consists of several days of tedium punctuated by an hour or two of sheer boredom

When rained-out anglers sit down to a game of cards, they never play "Go Fish"

If getting there is anywhere near half the fun, don't go

Murphy's FISHING LORE

The only really interesting fishing stories
are the ones told by the fish

There is an ounce of truth in every ten-pound trout

All whoppers began life as minnows

Fish put on weight when they escape

The key ingredients of a fish story are how big or how many the fish, how light the tackle, how long the fight, and how gullible the audience

To make a long story short, omit the part about the fish

The only thing you can learn from reading fishing books is that you can't learn anything from reading fishing books, but you have to read an awful lot of them to figure it out

The best time to tell a fellow angler about a secret hot fishing spot is at his funeral

Never ask the guy in the tackle shop if you need a new rod

Never take fishing tips from people with missing fingers

Everyone has the strength of character to watch another angler lose a fish

If at first you don't succeed, start working
on the story

Every fishing theory holds at least a
little water

Any change is for the worse, except
for underwear

$Give$ a man a fish, you give him heartburn for a day; teach a man to fish, you give him heartburn for a lifetime

The only really bad day of fishing is when there's nothing in the ice chest at the start of the trip, either

Ancient fishing wisdom:

Wind from the east, fish are least

Wind from the west, fish are at rest

Wind from the north, fish won't
venture forth

Wind from the south shuts a fish's mouth

There are two secrets of fishing:

1. Never tell another angler
the secret of fishing